Bring a Torch, Jeannette, Isabella

Trumpet 1

traditional French carol
arranged by Luther Henderson

T0039506

Ding Dong! Merrily On High

Trumpet 1
(Piccolo Tpt.)

traditional carol
arranged by Luther Henderson

Go Tell It On The Mountain

Trumpet 1

19th century Negro Spiritual
arranged by Luther Henderson

God Rest Ye Merry Gentlemen

Flügelhorn 1

traditional London carol, 19th century tune
arranged by Luther Henderson

Here We Come A-Wassailing

Trumpet 1
(Picc. Tpt. optional)

traditional carol from the north of England
arranged by Luther Henderson

The Huron Carol

Trumpet 1

traditional carol
arranged by Luther Henderson

I Saw Three Ships

Trumpet 1
(Picc.)

traditional English carol
arranged by Luther Henderson

Sussex Carol

Trumpet 1

traditional English carol
arranged by Luther Henderson